A new peacock-butterfly sits beside the empty case

Now it does not eat any more nettles but sucks in sap with its proboscis

After about two weeks it forces its way out and gradually unfolds its wings

ngs quite still. No one can see the caterpillar in the chrysalis anging into a butterfly

The last skin splits. Out comes the pupa looking like a tube

One day the caterpillar looks for a place where it can change into a pupa

The Snail

Every snail can lay eggs because it is both male and female at the same time. It digs a small hole in soft earth and lays about forty white eggs

Three weeks later the little snails come out of the egg shells. Their little shells are still thin and almost transparent

In the earth they find their first food—decayed plants. Also they nibble with their rasped tongues on the shell of the egg. This makes their shells harden and grow

Snails see and smell with both pairs of feelers. They can sense lettuce and strawberries from far away and crawl towards them leaving behind a trail of silvery slime

The snail has a bare, unprotected body which would dry up in the sun. So snails are usually found in the shade of bushes or under plants. If it is too dry for them outside, they draw back into their shells and seal them with a thin skin of slime

In autumn they close up their houses securely with a covering of slime. They lie there without eating or moving throughout winter until it gets warm again in spring

The River Trout

Most creatures spawn, hatch or give birth in spring or summer. Trout spawn in winter. They swim against the current of the river until they find a suitable place. There the female makes a hole with her tail in the shingle. She lays more than a thousand eggs (the spawn) which the male immediately fertilises. Then they both swim away

Some of the eggs are washed away and some are eaten by fish. So only some of the eggs develop undisturbed and hatch after about three months. The very young fish stays in his hiding-place and takes nourishment from his yolk sac which he has from birth

After a week he ventures out of his hiding-place. He must now search for food like insect larvae and worms. Soon the young trout is jumping for flies which dance on top of the water

The trout grows slowly. After a year he is still only ten centimetres long

The Chaffinch

As with many birds the female chaffinch is less colourful than the male. In spring she builds a very clever nest and disguises it well. The male sits by the nest and sings. His song means, "Here are beautiful chaffinches!" No others build their nest nearby

The female lays her eggs in the nest and begins to brood. She sits on the eggs and keeps them warm. Gradually a baby bird develops inside the egg. After two weeks he pecks the egg open from the inside and comes out, still naked and with his eyes shut

This family has five young and they all want to be fed all the time. For two weeks their parents have to fetch mosquitoes and beetles for the young

Every time the mother bird comes to the nest, she sees a row of open beaks. Then she must feed, feed, feed! When the young birds leave the nest, they start eating seed grains. At last the little chaffinches learn to fly and can look for food for themselves. But scarcely has the young family left the nest when the female starts to brood again

The Pond Frog

In early summer you will see female frogs carrying male frogs on their backs. When the female lays her eggs in a pond or a lake the male adds his seed to them. Only then can young frogs develop.

A female frog can lay as many as two thousand eggs, in clumps here and there. In the water the eggs swell, and in the transparent egg a small black spot can be seen. In a few days this turns into a small creature with a thick body and a long tail—a tadpole. The tadpole leaves the egg and looks on the stalks of water plants for algae to eat

The tadpole gets fatter and fatter. Eventually a pair o hind legs with a web between the toes grow beside the tail. Then front legs grow and the tadpole becomes a frog. Finally the tail shrivels up and disappears

At first the tadpole can breathe under water, through gills like a fish. Lungs are growing at the same time as the legs and the gills soon disappear. The frog has to put his head above water to breathe. When he goes after insects, he sometimes leaps high into the air

Tadpoles and frogs are eaten by many other animals. So the female lays many more eggs than will grow into frogs.

The Ring-snake

The ring-snake lives on land but likes to be near water. This is important because he likes to catch newts, frogs and small fish. He can swim and dive. He grabs his prey as quickly as lightning. Often the prey is bigger than the snake's body. He opens his mouth so wide that he can swallow his prey whole

In mid-summer the ring-snake looks for a good place to lay her eggs. It must be sheltered, warm and moist. Then when she has laid between fifteen and twenty-five eggs she slips away and forgets about them

The eggs do not have a hard shell, but a soft one more like a skin

After about two months, with the warmth of the sun and the ground, a small snake has developed inside the egg. It is about as long as a pencil when it finally slips out of the egg

Now it is autumn. The little snake looks for a place to spend the winter. There it stays in hibernation right through until spring

The Wood Mouse

There are almost as many wood mice as sparrows—but you will not see them very often as they are timid and nimble

They build their nests in dark hollows on the ground in woods, sometimes under the roots of trees. The nests are padded with hay and chewed-up straw

It is here that the mother mouse brings her young into the world. They have been growing in her womb until they almost look like mice. But when they are born they have no hair and their eyes are still shut